Nourishing Winter Meals planned by a Prudent Pensioner

A No Frills guide to getting the most from your budget

By Doreen Reed

I am grateful for many things in my life but I would say that being taught to sew, mend and eat well on a budget really had a positive impact on my personal contentment and well-being. Family and friends accept that I am not an organised person but planning meals ahead and wasting little has, for very many years, been second nature to me.

In this book, I show examples of planning main meals together with some of my well used recipes, I hope it will encourage and help anyone finding it difficult to cope on a tight budget.

I am not a well-known chef or celebrity, if I was, I would doubt that I would be so well experienced at working to a budget.

There are, of course, two ways to look at the cost of meals, to take a very simple example...

A poached egg on toast: As far as I am aware, it is not possible to buy one slice of bread one egg and a small amount of butter so you buy a sliced loaf which costs at least 60p there are possibly 15 slices so each slice costs 4p. You need to buy 250g of butter at £1.60p you would spread, say 5g on the toast, so approximate cost would be 3p. Eggs are sold in cartons of 6 costing say £1.50p, so each egg costs 25p so you could think the cost of a simple meal of poached egg on toast is 4p +3p+25p =32p but if the rest of the loaf, butter and eggs

1

are wasted then the actual cost of one poached egg on toast is
60p +£1.60p +£1.50p = £3.70p

To get the most from our budget we need to use all the ingredients, planning ahead is the best way to achieve this.

In this book I show how I plan ahead for 21 days of nourishing meals each recipe being for 2 adult portions. I achieve 42 nourishing main meals, a few soups and have stock in hand, for just under £90 (as at January 2018) that is £30 per week. My costings have been calculated using full prices; obviously money can be saved by taking advantage of the many offers. A young friend who has been trying out my recipes was delighted when she purchased some organic carrots for a few pence as they were just on the recommended use by date and made soup for her family for 25p.

I buy meat and free range eggs from my local butcher.

All my vegetable peelings go to compost.

For up to date news and recipes visit www.doreenreedpoet.com

and see the Prudent Pensioner's page.

Contents

Main meals   page

Soups cooked on the Hob

Soups cooked in a crockpot/slow cooker

Cakes and Puddings

Copyright

The Nourishing winter meals planned by a Prudent Pensioner

Dedications

To our dear Mother who managed so well on a low income and passed on her skills.

To the education system in the 1960's when domestic science/home economics was on the school curriculum.

My thanks to friends and family for trying my recipes.

My plan for day 1 and day 2 is Pork casserole with vegetables and mashed potatoes. For day 3 Vegetable bake with Egg and Bacon.

Shopping list days 1 - 3

Flat Mushrooms	£1.00
454g/1lb Pork cut into cubes	£3.40
Cabbage	£0.70
250g/8oz Butter	£1.60
Parsnips	£1.40
Carrots	£0.60
Potatoes	£2.00
Stock cubes chicken	£1.30
Stock cubes vegetable	£1.30
Shallots	£1.00
1litre sunflower oil	£1.20

(I buy sunflower oil as I also use it when making muffins)

Mature/vintage cheddar cheese 350g	£3.00
6 Eggs	£1.50
Salt	£0.40
Pepper	£1.00
Cornflour	£1.30
2 rashers back bacon	£1.20
Total	£23.90p

Day 1

I begin pork casserole at least 2 hours before we wish to eat. I usually cook double the quantity of meat and stock then either re heat it the following day or freeze it for another time. I hope when you have tried this you will agree the flavour is even better on the second serving.

SERVES 2 plus meat for 2 more portions
Cooked in Crockpot or Slow cooker for 90 minutes

Chicken or Vegetable stock cube
454g/1lb Pork cut in approximately 1" cubes
1 Flat Mushroom washed and sliced
2 med Shallots peeled and thinly sliced
2 med Carrots peeled and sliced
2 med Parsnips peeled and sliced
A little Cooking oil
Cornflour
Salt and Pepper
Potatoes approx. 180g/6oz per adult
Butter

Turn Crockpot on to high setting. Boil up a kettle of water and pour approx. 500ml hot water into crockpot, leave covered for 5 mins. Dissolve stock cube in 500 ml of hot water, carefully taste and season if necessary. I find most stock cubes have a good flavour but I have had the occasional bland one which, of course would not give the desired tasty results. Empty out water from crockpot and replace with hot stock. You may want to count the number of pork cubes to make it easier to divide later.

Put oil in frying pan and lightly brown pork cubes on all sides then add this to stock in crockpot together with shallots mushroom, carrots and parsnips. Stir. Leave covered cooking for 90 mins. Can be turned down to lower setting after an hour but must be simmering well.

After an hour you may like to prepare potatoes: peel and cut into pieces, place in a saucepan in lightly salted water, bring to boil, reduce heat and let simmer for 5 minutes then turn off heat.

Check that meat is tender, cook longer if necessary and season if required. Reheat potatoes in water to boiling point; reduce heat and leave to simmer until cooked.

Using a warmed jug take out required amount of stock for gravy, from crockpot and pour into a saucepan. Over a medium heat thicken this to liking, with cornflour. (Approx. 1 dessertspoon cornflour mixed to a paste and poured gradually into stock, stirring continuously until thickened,) reduce heat and let simmer for 2 mins, stirring occasionally.

Strain water off potatoes and mash with a knob of butter.

Serve as much of the veg as required but only half the meat, keep the other half in crockpot, (turned off) in remaining stock, leave to cool then put in covered dish and refrigerate for next day.

You may have purchased a pack of 3 or 4 flat mushrooms, if so discard cling film and cover the remaining mushrooms with a kitchen towel and refrigerate, these will be used on Day 4.

Day 2

Pork casserole with vegetables, mashed potatoes and savoy cabbage

In readiness for the vegetable bake I plan for day 3, I will cook and mash twice as many potatoes as we need for this meal. I will also cook twice as many carrots, parsnips and cabbage as we need. I usually steam cook vegetables but they do cook just as well in a saucepan of lightly salted water. Use half or a little more if preferred, of savoy cabbage. Refrigerate piece not being used. Cut and slice the leaves thinly, place in a bowl of lightly salted cold water leave for 5 minutes, then rinse and place in a saucepan of lightly salted water, bring to boil, reduce heat, it takes only 5 minutes or so to cook so do this when carrots are beginning to soften.

While vegetables are cooking put meat and stock saved from Day 1 into a saucepan and bring to the boil, reduce heat, mix cornflour and water to a thin paste and gently stir into stock. Stir until thickened increasing heat if necessary. Stir and cook for 2 minutes. Check meat is piping hot, cook a little longer if necessary. Serve with half of the potatoes, carrots, parsnips and cabbage. Put the spare veg into a bowl or a saucepan, cover and leave aside until later.

Later, I will mash the carrots and parsnips and mix well with potatoes and cabbage and place in a lightly buttered oven proof dish covered and refrigerated until next day.

Day 3

Vegetable Bake with fried egg and a rasher of back bacon.

As well as vegetables in dish from day 2 you will need

70g/3oz. of mature cheddar cheese grated

2 Eggs

2 rashers of Bacon

A little oil for frying

Preheat oven to oven to 200c/400f

Sprinkle grated cheese evenly over vegetable mix. Place dish, preferably on a baking tray, in preheated oven for 30 mins or until evenly browned.

Fry egg and bacon and serve with vegetable bake on warmed plates.

Note: *Bacon could also be cooked in oven in a lightly greased ovenproof dish, cook for 10-15 minutes turning after 7 minutes.*

My plan for day 4 is Minced Steak with Cauliflower and potatoes, for day 5 I plan Cheese and Onion Puddings with Cauliflower and potatoes and for day 6 Chicken Curry.

Shopping list days 4-6

with shallots, cooking oil, mushrooms, cornflour, potatoes, cheese and eggs already in stock, shopping needed is:

230g/8oz Minced Steak	£1.75
Plain flour	£1.30
Cauliflower	£1.00
White med sliced loaf	£0.60
Beef Stock cubes	£1.50
Jar of chutney	£1.50
Medium curry powder	£1.00
Long grain rice	£1.10
	£9.75

230g/8oz Chicken Breast best bought fresh on day 5 or 6

	£2.10
Total	£11.85

A tablespoon of milk will also be needed on day 5.

DAY 4

Minced Steak with cauliflower and potatoes Serves 2.

230g/8oz Minced Steak

2 Shallots

A little cooking oil

Flat Mushroom(s) from Day 1

Flour approx. 2 rounded teaspoons

Cornflour

Beef stock cube

Potatoes approx. 180g/6oz per adult

1 Cauliflower

Peel potatoes, cut into pieces and cook in lightly salted water. Dissolve stock cube in 500ml. hot water and put in a saucepan. Peel and slice shallots and add half to stock, clean and cut mushroom(s) each into 8 pieces add to stock, bring to boil then reduce heat, cover and leave to simmer. Check potatoes are soft, cook a little longer if necessary, then turn off heat and leave in saucepan. Using half of the cauliflower, trim off and discard base of stalk. Cut into 4 pieces, place in a bowl in lightly salted cold water leave for 5 minutes. Then rinse and place in a saucepan of lightly salted water, bring to boil, reduce heat, cover and leave to simmer gently for 10 minutes, when, if cooked, turn off heat. Refrigerate other half of cauliflower.

Then cook meat: Put approximately 1 teaspoon of oil in another saucepan turn heat to medium, add rest of sliced shallot and minced steak and stir to break it up, continue stirring and turning meat over to cook evenly, this will not take long. When browned all over add flour, mix thoroughly then add approx. 230ml of stock stir and cook for 2 mins, add mushrooms and a little stock from other saucepan then it is ready to serve. Mix cornflour and water to a thin paste and gently stir into stock in other saucepan, stir until thickened increasing heat if necessary, this makes nice gravy. Bring water in potatoes to boiling point then strain off and mash with a knob of butter.

Check cauliflower is cooked, if so, strain off water and serve.

DAY 5

Cheese and Onion puddings with cauliflower and mashed potatoes.

180g/6oz Strong flavoured Cheddar Cheese grated

1 Shallot sliced thinly

1½ medium slices white bread (preferably a little stale) crusts removed

2 Eggs beaten with I tbsp. milk seasoned lightly

Potatoes approx. 180g/6oz per adult

Cauliflower from Day 4

Butter for greasing

Pre heat oven to 190c/375f

Grease 2 ramekin dishes or you could put all in one dish and divide up.

Make bread into (not too fine) crumbs, put into mixing bowl, add cheese and sliced shallot and mix in.

Add beaten eggs and milk and mix well. Put mixture into greased ramekin dishes and place on a baking tray in pre heated oven and cook for 35-45 mins, when they should be nicely risen.

While Cheese and onion savoury puddings are cooking, peel potatoes, cut into pieces and put into a saucepan of lightly salted water, bring to boil and simmer for 10 minutes, if they are then beginning to soften turn off heat and leave covered. Take the half of cauliflower from refrigerator, trim off and discard base of stalk. Cut into 4 pieces, place in lightly salted cold water leave for 5 minutes, then rinse and place in a saucepan of lightly salted water, bring to boil, reduce heat, cover and leave to simmer gently for 10 minutes, or until cooked, then turn off heat.

When Cheese and onion savoury puddings are ready, turn off oven but leave them in while you reheat water in potatoes to boiling point, then turn off heat, drain and mash with a knob of butter. Reheat water in cauliflower to boiling point, and then turn off heat and drain off water.

This is all now ready to serve and enjoy.

DAY 6

Chicken Curry Serves 2.

230g/8oz Chicken Breast cut into small pieces (approximately 20)

Med Shallot sliced thinly

2 dessert spoons cooking Oil

1 dessertspoon of Chutney

1 teaspoon of medium Curry powder (adjust to suit personal taste, this isn't too hot)

1 dessert spoon Cornflour

Chicken stock cube dissolved in 500ml of hot water.

120g/4oz Long grain rice

Put 1/3rd oil in frying pan over medium heat, add curry powder and sliced shallot, mix and fry gently for 2 minutes, stirring constantly. Remove from frying pan and place in a saucepan with all of stock, bring to boil. Reduce heat and keep simmering gently. Add rest of oil to frying pan over a medium heat; add chicken pieces and stirring constantly, lightly fry on all sides. Transfer to stock in saucepan adding chutney. Bring to boil, then reduce heat and simmer gently, this will take approx. 15 mins so meanwhile cook rice following instructions on packet.

When chicken is cooked through, in a jug, add a little water to cornflour and mix to a thin paste, gradually pour into stock stirring until thickened. Serve chicken and sauce on a bed of rice.

My Plan for day 7 is Beef sausages with gravy, mashed potatoes and broccoli, for days 8 and 9 I plan Beef casserole with vegetables I do have a couple of carrots in my cupboard; I will make soup with those.

Shopping list for days 7-9

With shallots, cooking oil, cornflour, a few potatoes, stock cubes already in stock, shopping needed is:

4 Beef sausages	£2.50
Parsnips	£1.00
Broccoli	£0.50
Shallots	£1.00
454g/1lb Braising steak cut into cubes	£5.50
Flat mushrooms	£1.00
Carrots	£0.60
Potatoes 2.5g	£2.00
	£14.10

DAY 7

Beef Sausages, onion gravy, mashed potatoes and broccoli.

4 Beef sausages

Beef Stock cube

Broccoli 330g/12oz

1 medium or 2 small Shallots (more if liked)

Cornflour

Potatoes approx. 180g/6oz per adult

Cut Broccoli into florets and place in a bowl of lightly salted cold water. Peel potatoes and cut into pieces, place in a saucepan of lightly salted water, cover and bring to boil then reduce heat and leave simmering until cooked then turn off heat, it is best to check after 15 minutes as some potatoes cook much quicker than others, to mash nicely it is important that they are not too soft.
In a saucepan dissolve stock cube in 400ml hot water. Peel and slice shallot and add to stock.

Rinse Broccoli florets well. Cook in lightly salted boiling water, should take approximately 10 minutes.
Turn grill to high setting. Place sausages in grill pan, with a sharp knife make 2 small slits on 2 sides of each one, place pan under grill, turn sausages over after a few minutes to cook evenly, repeat a few times until browning on each side, reduce heat a little and leave for a

few minutes still turning sausages until thoroughly cooked, turn off grill and keep them warm.

Over a medium heat thicken gravy to liking, with cornflour. Approx. 1 dessertspoon cornflour mixed to a paste and poured gradually into stock, stirring continuously until thickened, reduce heat and let simmer for 2 mins, stirring occasionally.

Mash potatoes when they are cooked, strain water off broccoli and serve.

Note: *stalk of broccoli could be saved and trimmed and peeled and cut into small pieces and added to casserole on Day 8 or used in soup.*

Day 8

Beef Casserole with vegetables and mashed potatoes.
SERVES 2 plus meat for 2 more portions.
Cooked in Crockpot or Slow cooker for 2 hours, longer if necessary.

Beef stock cube
454g/1lb braising steak cut in approximately 1" cubes
1 or 2 Flat Mushrooms
2 med Shallots
2 med Carrots
2 med Parsnips
A little cooking oil
Cornflour
Salt and Pepper
Potatoes approx. 180g/6oz per adult

Turn Crockpot on to high setting. Boil up a kettle of water and pour approx. 500ml hot water into crockpot, leave covered for five minutes. Dissolve stock cube in 500 ml in jug of hot water. Empty out water from crockpot and replace with hot stock.

Peel and thinly slice shallots, carrots and parsnips. Wash and cut mushrooms each into 6 or 8 pieces, leave to one side. If broccoli stalk saved from day 7, trim, peel and cut into small pieces.

You may want to count the number of beef cubes to make it easier to divide later.

Put oil in frying pan and lightly brown beef cubes on all sides then add this to stock in crockpot together with shallots mushroom, carrots, parsnips and broccoli stalk if used and stir. Leave covered cooking for

2 hours. Heat can be turned down to medium setting after an hour but must be simmering well.

After 90 minutes you may like to prepare potatoes: peel and cut into pieces, place in a saucepan in lightly salted water, bring to boil, reduce heat and let simmer for 5 minutes then turn off heat. Check that meat is tender cook longer if necessary season if required. When meat is tender reheat potatoes in water to boiling point; reduce heat and leave to simmer until cooked.

Using warmed jug take out required amount of stock for gravy, from crockpot and pour into a saucepan. Over a medium heat thicken this to liking with cornflour. (Approx. 1 dessertspoon cornflour mixed to a paste and poured gradually into stock, stirring continuously until thickened, reduce heat and let simmer for 2 mins, stirring occasionally.)

Strain water off potatoes and mash with a knob of butter.

Serve amount of veg required but only half the meat, keep the other half in crockpot, (turned off) in remaining stock, leave to cool then put in a covered dish and refrigerate for next day.

Day 9

Beef Casserole with vegetables and mashed potatoes.

1 med Carrot peeled and sliced

1 med Parsnip peeled and sliced

Cornflour approx. 1 dessert spoon

Salt and Pepper

Potatoes approx. 180g/6oz per adult

Beef saved from Day 8

Peel and cut potatoes into pieces, place in a saucepan in lightly salted water, bring to boil, reduce heat and leave to simmer until cooked.

Place carrot in a saucepan in lightly salted water, bring to boil, reduce heat and leave to simmer until cooked.

Place parsnip in a saucepan in lightly salted water, bring to boil, reduce heat and leave to simmer until cooked. Parsnips do not usually take more than 5 or 10 minutes to cook.

While vegetables are cooking put meat and stock saved from day 8 into a saucepan and bring to the boil, reduce heat, simmer for 5 minutes, it should be piping hot. Mix cornflour and water to a thin paste and gently stir into stock. Stir until thickened increasing heat if necessary. Stir and cook for 2 minutes.

Strain water off vegetables when cooked; add butter to potatoes and mash. Serve meat with potatoes, carrot and parsnip.

My plan for day 10 is Bacon & Mushroom Risotto, day 11 Herby Pork Loaf with potatoes and Brussel Sprouts and day 12 Cottage Pie with gravy.

Shopping list for days 10 - 12

With shallots, cooking oil, cornflour potatoes and stock cubes already in stock, shopping needed is:

2 rashers Back Bacon	£1.00
500g Risotto rice	£1.25
Flat mushrooms	£1.00
230g/8oz Minced Pork	£1.85
Rolled oats 500g	£0.80
Brussel Sprouts	£0.50
230g/8oz Minced Steak	£1.75
Mustard powder 100g	£1.40
Dried mixed herbs	£1.00
	£10.55

Day 10

Bacon and Mushroom Risotto.

Serves 2.

1 Teaspoon of cooking oil

Small piece of butter (about the size of a walnut)

2 Rashers of Back Bacon

1 medium size Shallot

130g/5oz Risotto Rice

2 Flat mushrooms

1 Chicken stock cube

In a medium size saucepan dissolve stock cube in 500ml hot water. Peel and slice shallot add to stock. Clean and cut each mushroom into 8 pieces then add to stock. Bring to boil, reduce heat and leave to simmer gently.

Cut bacon into strips approximately 30mm x 20 mm or 1" by ¾". Put butter and oil in a medium size saucepan and over a low heat add bacon and cook stirring constantly.

Add rice stir for 2 minutes then add stock, shallot and mushrooms, bring to boil, stir well. Reduce heat and leave to simmer, covered, stirring occasionally, for 20 - 25 mins or until rice is tender. It is then ready to serve and enjoy.

Day 11

Herby Pork loaf, mashed potatoes and Brussel Sprouts.

Makes 2 generous portions.

1 Tablespoon milk

1 Egg

35g/1½oz Rolled Oats

230g/8oz Minced Pork

Medium size shallot sliced thinly

A little mustard powder

1 Teaspoon dried mixed herbs

Salt and pepper

Potatoes approx... 180g/6oz per adult

Chicken stock cube

Cornflour

Large knob of butter

12 Brussel Sprouts (more or less if preferred)

In a mixing bowl beat egg and milk together, add oats, mix well then leave to soak for 30 minutes.

Pre heat oven to 190c/375f.

Add pork, shallot, mustard powder, dried herbs and a little salt and pepper to oats and mix well. Place in a lightly greased loaf tin, or make into a loaf shape and place on lightly greased baking tray or other suitable ovenproof dish. Bake in pre heated oven for 30 minutes or until brown and crispy on outside.

Meanwhile: peel potatoes and cut into pieces, place in a saucepan in lightly salted water, bring to boil, reduce heat and leave to simmer until cooked.

Remove outer leaves from Brussel sprouts and discard, cut off any excess stalk. Rinse in cold water then drop into a saucepan of lightly salted boiling water, leave to simmer for 6 minutes, turn off heat.

To make gravy: In a saucepan, dissolve stock cube in 300 ml of hot water. Over a medium heat thicken this to liking, with cornflour. (Approx. 1 dessertspoon cornflour mixed to a paste and poured gradually into stock, stirring continuously until thickened,) reduce heat and let simmer for 2 mins, stirring occasionally.

When meat loaf is cooked, reheat water in potatoes and sprouts to boiling. Insert knife into sprouts if not cooked simmer for a few more minutes. Turn off heat. Drain water off potatoes and mash with a knob of butter.

Drain water off sprouts, this is now ready to serve and enjoy.

Earlier in the day I will make a Cottage pie, this will be ready for day 12. I can put it in the oven with the Herby Pork Loaf; it tastes even nicer when reheated the following day.

Day 12

If pie was made day 11, it just needs reheating in oven or microwave; it should be piping hot before serving.

To make gravy, heat the stock in a saucepan. In a jug or cup mix cornflour and cold water to make a fairly thin paste, gradually add this to stock stirring continuously, bring to boil, reduce heat and cook for a further 2 minutes. Serve with hot cottage pie.

Cottage Pie   Makes 2 generous portions.

230g/8oz Minced steak

1 medium size Shallot peeled and sliced

1 medium size Carrot peeled and cut into small pieces

1 small Parsnip peeled and cut into small pieces

1 Beef stock cube

1 dessert spoon Plain flour

1 level teaspoon dried mixed herbs

600g/1¼ lbs Potatoes

Knob of Butter

50g/2oz mature Cheddar Cheese grated

1 dessert spoon Cornflour

Salt and pepper

You will need 750ml/1½ pint ovenproof dish.

Peel potatoes and cut into pieces, place in a saucepan of lightly salted water, cover bring to boil then reduce heat and leave simmering until cooked then turn off heat, it is best to check after 15 minutes as some potatoes cook much quicker than others, to mash nicely it is important they are not too soft.

Dissolve stock cube in 400ml hot water.

Turn on oven to 190c/375f (if being cooked immediately).

In another saucepan, over a low-medium heat, gently dry fry shallot, minced steak, carrot and parsnip, stirring often, for approximately 4 minutes when meat should be gently browning. Stir in herbs and plain flour. Mix well then gradually add 250ml of the stock bring to boil and stir until thickened, season with salt and pepper if necessary. Turn off heat and transfer mince mixture to oven proof dish. Put remaining stock into this saucepan, stir to loosen any bits of meat and vegetable this will make tastier gravy.

If pie is not going to be eaten within a couple of hours, pour remaining stock into a jug, cover and leave to cool then refrigerate.

When potatoes are cooked drain off the water, add butter and half of the grated cheese and mash well.

Spread mashed potatoes evenly over mince mix, sprinkle with remaining cheese. Bake in pre heated oven for 25 minutes. It should be nicely golden on top. If pie is not going to be eaten until next day, cover and leave to cool then refrigerate.

To make additional gravy, heat the remaining stock in the saucepan. In a jug or cup mix cornflour and cold water to make a fairly thin paste, gradually add this to stock stirring continuously, bring to boil, reduce heat and cook for a further 2 minutes.

My plan for day 13 is Macaroni Cheese with cauliflower and day 14 Cauliflower and Potato soup.

Shopping list days 13-14

With bread, potatoes, butter and plain flour in stock.

Dried Macaroni Pasta 500g	£0.85
Milk	£1.10
Mature Cheddar Cheese 350g	£3.00
Cauliflower	£1.00
	£5.95

Day 13

Macaroni Cheese with cauliflower serves 2.

150g/6oz Dried macaroni pasta

15g/½oz Butter

15g/½oz Plain flour

250ml/½ pint Milk

1/4 teaspoon English mustard

100g/4oz Strong flavoured Cheddar Cheese grated

Salt &Pepper

1/2 Cauliflower (about 350g/12oz.) cut into florets and soaked in lightly salted water for 5 minutes.

You will need a 850ml/1½ pint ovenproof dish.

Bring a medium size saucepan of lightly salted water to the boil. Rinse cauliflower florets in cold water then add to the hot water. When water is boiling again, reduce heat and simmer until tender (about 5) minutes, don't overcook. Strain off water, place Florets in an ovenproof dish spread evenly. Cover and put aside. Rinse saucepan, refill with more lightly salted water bring to boil then add the macaroni. Boil for 5 minutes then drain.

Meanwhile melt butter in a saucepan, add flour beating quickly to form a smooth base for the sauce. Whisk in milk a little at a time until all mixed then bring to the boil still stirring constantly. Reduce heat to simmer, stir in mustard and salt and pepper to taste. Cook for 2 minutes stirring often. Add par cooked macaroni to pan, stir and cook for 4 minutes. The starches in the pasta will thicken the sauce as it cooks.

Preheat grill to medium. Remove sauce from heat and stir in 2/3rd of the cheese.

Pour sauce over cauliflower, spreading evenly. Sprinkle over remaining cheese and grill for approximately 6 minutes or until cheese is browned and sauce is bubbling.

Note:

Mixing mustard powder in with flour can help to avoid lumps.

Boiling water in kettle then pouring into saucepan saves a little time.

Day 14

Cauliflower soup serves 2.

Cauliflower left from Day 13

1 medium size Shallot

1 medium size Potato

Chicken or vegetable stock cube dissolved in 500ml hot water

Knob of butter

Salt and pepper

Trim off discoloured base of cauliflower and any outside leaves and discard. Cut off florets and place together with stalk in a bowl of lightly salted cold water. Cut any clean leaves from smaller stalks and add these and the stalks to the water leave to soak for a few minutes.

Peel potato and cut into small pieces.

Peel shallot and slice.

Take stalks from water, rinse and cut into small pieces.

Put butter into a saucepan and soften over a medium heat add potato and stalk pieces and shallot and stir well. Cook for 3 minutes stirring frequently, rinse florets and leaves, add to saucepan with stock and stir well. Bring to the boil then reduce heat, cover and leave simmering for 15 minutes or until potato and cauliflower are soft. Add more seasoning if necessary. Strain off liquid into a jug, put potato and cauliflower mix into a suitable jug or bowl and whizz with blender until well mixed and smooth. Put mix back into saucepan; carefully add in stock from jug stirring until smooth. Reheat, then it is ready to serve and enjoy. Serve with cheese sandwiches or fingers of cheese on toast.

My plan for day 15 is Chicken in Cider sauce with mushrooms, for day 16 I plan Chicken, Mushroom and Celery risotto, for day 17 a Curried Minced Steak with rice and day 18 Grilled Pork Steaks with cauliflower and braised celery.

Shopping list for days 15-18

With potatoes, stock cubes, shallots, plain flour and milk in stock.

2 x 230g/8oz Chicken Breasts	£4.20
Bottle dry cider 500ml	£1.90
Closed cup or button mushrooms 500g	£1.40
Celery	£0.55
Cauliflower	£1.00
Potatoes 2.5kg	£2.15
	£11.20

Meat is best purchased on Day 17

Minced Steak 230g/8oz	£1.75
2 x 170g/6oz Pork steaks	£2.50
	£15.45

Day 15

Chicken in Cider sauce with Mushrooms and Celery Serves 2.

230g/8oz Chicken breasts cut into approximately 20 pieces.

Dry Cider you will need a stopper to seal bottle to save half for day 16.

A few Button Mushrooms trimmed, wiped with damp cloth and cut in halves.

250ml/½ pint Milk

25g/1oz. Butter

25g/1oz. Plain flour

Small Shallot peeled and thinly sliced

Potatoes

3 or 4 sticks of Celery

Peel potatoes, cut into pieces and cook in a saucepan of lightly salted water.

Pour 250 ml (½ pint) of the Cider into a saucepan. (Reseal bottle with a stopper and refrigerate for day 16.) Add shallot and chicken pieces turn heat to high until cider is boiling, reduce heat and leave covered simmering gently for 10-15 minutes or until chicken is thoroughly cooked adding mushrooms for the last 5 minutes.

Meanwhile trim and clean celery and cut each stick into 3 or 4 pieces, put into a saucepan in lightly salted water, bring to boil, reduce heat, cover and simmer until cooked to taste, this will only take a few minutes.

When chicken is cooked prepare sauce. Strain off 125ml /¼ pint of cider and add to milk leaving chicken and mushrooms in remainder. Melt butter in a saucepan; add flour beating quickly to form a smooth base for the sauce, whisk in milk and cider a little at a time until all mixed then bring to the boil still stirring constantly. Reduce heat to simmer, add salt and pepper to taste. Cook for 3 minutes stirring often.

When sauce is ready, mash potatoes, strain off liquid from chicken and serve chicken and mushroom in the sauce with potatoes and celery.

Note:
Small pieces of fried streaky bacon mixed with celery adds a nice flavour.

Day 16

Chicken, Mushroom and Celery risotto. Serves 2.

230g/8oz Chicken Breast cut into about 30 pieces.

Medium Shallot

Mushrooms

2 large or 3 small sticks of Celery

130g/4ozRisotto rice

Chicken stock cube

230ml/7fl.oz Cider from day 15

Knob of Butter about half the size of a walnut

Teaspoon cooking oil

Dissolve stock cube in 500ml/1 pint hot water put this into a saucepan, add chicken pieces and bring to boil, reduce heat, cover and leave gently simmering for 10 minutes or until chicken is cooked thoroughly.

In a medium size saucepan, over a low heat, add butter and oil. When butter is softened, add rice and stir well. Increase heat a little and stirring gently let rice cook for 2 minutes. Carefully add cider and stir, add 2/3rds.stock stir well. Cover and leave simmering. Clean mushrooms and slice each one into 4 add to saucepan.Trim and clean celery, cut into pieces approx.20cm (1 inch) in length, add to saucepan and stir well. You may need to increase heat a little until contents is simmering gently, adjust heat if necessary, cover and leave simmering for 10 mins then add the rest of stock with chicken and simmer for a further 10mins or until rice is tender. This is ready to serve and enjoy.

Day 17

(Mild) Curried Minced steak with rice.

Serves 2.

230g/8oz Minced Steak

Medium size Shallot peeled and thinly sliced

Beef or vegetable stock cube

Plain flour

Curry powder medium

1 Dessert spoon of chutney

In a jug dissolve stock cube in 400ml of hot water.

Over a low to medium heat, dry fry meat and shallot, stirring and turning constantly to allow it to brown evenly. Add chutney and mix well. Carefully stir in half of the stock. Mix together a dessert spoon of flour and a rounded teaspoon (more if liked) of curry powder, stir in sufficient cold water to mix to a thin paste add this to meat, stir well and cook for a further 5 minutes, stirring frequently. Add more stock if necessary, leave on low heat, stirring occasionally while you cook the rice following instructions on packet.

Day 18

Grilled Pork Steaks with mashed potatoes, cauliflower and braised celery.

Serves 2.

2 Pork Steaks160-180g/6-7oz

Medium size Cauliflower

2 large or 3 small sticks of Celery

Chicken or vegetable stock cube dissolved in 400ml hot water.

Cornflour

A little oil

3 knobs of Butter

Potatoes approx. 720g/24oz allowing for quantity to be saved for Cauliflower and Celery Bake for day 19.

Using 1/3rd. of the cauliflower, cut off florets leaving a little stalk on each, place in a bowl of lightly salted water and leave while you prepare potatoes: Peel potatoes, cut into pieces and place in a saucepan of lightly salted water, bring to the boil and leave to simmer gently. Check after 15 minutes, if soft turn off heat and leave in hot water.

Turn grill to high, wipe pork steaks with clean damp kitchen towel and place them on the grill tray, Smear each one with approximately ½ teaspoon of oil, place under pre heated grill and leave for 2-3 minutes, then turn them over and grill on other side for 2-3 minutes. Reduce heat by one setting and continue to cook, turning them over occasionally to allow even grilling for a further 10-15 minutes, or until thoroughly cooked. Keep warm until vegetables are ready. Meanwhile rinse cauliflower florets in cold water, drain and place in a saucepan in lightly salted boiling water. Wash celery and cut each stick into 8 pieces, place celery pieces on top of florets and leave to simmer for 10 minutes or until cooked to liking.

To make gravy place stock in a saucepan, mix a dessert spoon of cornflour with cold water to make a thin paste, add to stock stirring well, bring to the boil, reduce heat and leave to simmer for 2-3 minutes.

Strain off potatoes and mash with butter. Reserve half for Day 19.

Strain off cauliflower florets and celery.

Serve pork steaks with mashed potatoes, cauliflower and braised celery.

My plan for day 19 is Pork sausages with Celery and Cauliflower bake, day 20 Macaroni Cheese with leek and day 21 Herby Meat Loaf with potatoes and cauliflower.

Shopping list for days19-21

Having checked my stock cupboard I just need:

6 Eggs	£1.50
Celery	£0.55
Cauliflower	£1.00
4 Pork Sausages	£2.30
Minced Steak 230g/8oz (Best purchased day 21)	£1.75
Leek 230g/8oz	£0.50
	£7.60

Day 19

Pork Sausages and Cauliflower and Celery bake.

Serves 2.

4 Pork Sausages

Potatoes (cooked and mashed day 18)

2 sticks of Celery

1/3rd of a medium size Cauliflower

60g/2oz mature Cheese grated

Firstly make Cauliflower and Celery bake:

You will need a lightly buttered ovenproof dish approx. ¾ litre.

Trim discoloured base from cauliflower, cut off florets, cut bits of stalk into smaller pieces, place in a bowl of lightly salted water and leave for 5 minutes Wash celery and cut each stick into 8 pieces, strain water off cauliflower and rinse well. If cooking immediately pre heat oven to 200c/400f.

Steam or cook cauliflower and celery in hot water for 10 mins, celery and cauliflower should be partly cooked. Strain off water. Mash bits of stalk with mashed potato, slice celery thinly. Stir celery slices into mashed potatoes, then mix in florets and half of the grated cheese. Place mix into the ovenproof dish, sprinkle over remaining cheese. Bake in pre heated oven for 25-30 mins or until nicely golden.

After 20 minutes turn grill to high setting. Place sausages in grill pan. With a sharp knife make 2 small slits on 2 sides of each one, place pan under grill, turn sausages over after a few minutes to cook evenly, repeat a few times until browning on each side, reduce heat a little and cook, still turning sausages, until thoroughly cooked, turn off grill and keep them warm. Serve with Cauliflower and Celery bake.

Day 20

Macaroni Cheese with Leek.

Serves 2.

150g/5oz Dried Macaroni pasta

25g/1oz Butter

25g/1oz Plain flour

300ml/1/2 pint Milk

1/4 teaspoon English mustard

100g/4oz strong flavoured Cheddar Cheese grated

Salt &Pepper

230g/8oz Leek sliced

You will need a 850ml/1½ pint ovenproof dish.

Put leek slices in a colander and rinse with cold water then transfer them to a saucepan and add the milk, carefully bring to the boil, reduce heat and simmer until leeks are tender.

Bring a medium size saucepan of salted water to the boil add the macaroni boil for 5 minutes then drain.

Remove leek slices from milk and place in an ovenproof dish spreading evenly.

Mix mustard powder into flour. Melt butter in a saucepan; add flour and mustard powder beating quickly to form a smooth base for the sauce. Whisk in milk a little at a time until all mixed then bring to the boil still stirring constantly. Reduce heat to simmer, Add salt and pepper to taste. Cook for 2 minutes stirring often. Add par cooked macaroni to pan, stir and cook for 4 minutes. The starches in the pasta will thicken the sauce as it cooks.

Preheat grill to medium.

Remove sauce from heat and stir in 2/3rd of the cheese. Pour sauce over leeks, spreading evenly. Sprinkle over remaining cheese and grill for approximately 6 minutes or until cheese is browned and sauce is bubbling.

Day 21

Herby Meat loaf, mashed potatoes and cauliflower.

Makes 2 generous portions.

1 Tablespoon milk

1 Egg

35g/1½oz Rolled oats

230g/8oz Minced steak

Medium size shallot sliced thinly

A little Mustard powder

1 Teaspoon dried mixed herbs

Salt and pepper

Potatoes

1/3rd cauliflower from day 20

In a mixing bowl beat egg and milk together, add oats, mix well then leave to soak for 30 minutes.

Pre heat oven to 190c/375f

Add minced steak, shallot, mustard powder, dried herbs and a little salt and pepper to oats and mix well. Place in a lightly greased loaf tin, or make into a loaf shape and place on lightly greased baking tray or other suitable ovenproof dish. Bake in pre heated oven for 30 minutes or until brown and crispy on outside.

Meanwhile trim discoloured base from cauliflower, cut into pieces, place in a bowl of lightly salted water and leave for 5 minutes. Peel potatoes and cut into pieces and cook in lightly salted water. Rinse cauliflower and put in another saucepan in lightly salted water, bring to the boil, then reduce heat and leave to simmer, check after 10 minutes, if cooked then turn off heat and leave in hot water until needed.

When meat loaf is cooked, reheat water in potatoes and cauliflower to boiling. Turn off heat, drain and mash potatoes, drain water off cauliflower, this is now ready to serve and enjoy.

Summary of cost of shopping:

Days 1 - 3	23.90
Days 4 - 6	11.85
Days 7 - 9	14.10
Days 10 - 12	10.55
Days 13 -14	5.95
Days 15 -18	15.45
Days 19 - 21	<u>7.60</u>
Total	£89.40

I still have in hand, potatoes, stock cubes, sunflower oil, cornflour, plain flour, chutney, risotto rice, mixed herbs, mustard powder, macaroni pasta, and curry powder. I have eaten the cheese on toast and I have had the rolled oats for breakfast.

Soups

Are always welcome in the cold weather; here are some of my favourite, nourishing, inexpensive, and simple to make soup recipes, a wise way of using up spare vegetables too.

These recipes make 2 generous portions.

I have also shown how I make vegetable soup in my crockpot on the days when I wish to prepare well in advance and get on with other things while it is cooking gently. On colder days too it is nice to have that little extra warmth in the kitchen.

A blender is a very useful gadget to have for soup making, if you do have to manage without one; a potato masher is useful, hopefully, when you turn out tasty soup, someone just may buy you a blender. Back in my schooldays we were taught to make potato and onion soup and we used a sieve.

Beef and vegetable soup.

50g/2oz Minced Steak

1 medium size Carrot

1 medium size Shallot

1 medium size Parsnip

1 medium size Potato

Beef or vegetable stock cube

Trim off tops and bottoms of vegetables, peel and cut into small pieces.

Dissolve stock cube in 500 ml of hot water.

Dry fry minced steak for a few minutes stirring constantly breaking it up.

Remove the cooked minced steak from the saucepan, cover and keep to one side. Don't worry that you cannot get all of meat from saucepan.

Stir in vegetables mix well add stock bring to boil reduce heat and simmer for 20 minutes, or until vegetables are soft.

Strain off most of liquid into a jug, put aside while you either put vegetables into liquidiser or use hand blender and whizz for a couple of minutes, alternatively use potato masher and mash well. Return liquid, 1/3rd at a time, to pureed vegetables in saucepan, stirring gently to mix well. Taste and add salt and pepper if required. When all liquid mixed in, add cooked minced steak, reheat to boiling point stirring gently. Turn off heat and enjoy.

Carrot soup cooked on the hob.

1 medium Shallot
15g/½oz Butter
Potato approx. 100g/4oz
Carrots approx. 230g/8oz
Chicken or vegetable stock cube dissolved in 500ml hot water.
Salt and Pepper to taste.

Peel potato and carrots and cut them up into small pieces.
Peel shallot and slice.
Place butter in a saucepan over a medium heat, add vegetables stir and mix well. Add stock, increase heat and bring to boiling point. Reduce heat and leave, covered, simmering gently, stirring occasionally, until vegetables are quite soft (approximately 15-20 minutes). Strain off most of the liquid into a jug, put aside while you either put vegetables into liquidiser or use a hand blender and whizz for a couple of minutes, alternatively use potato masher and mash well. Return liquid, 1/3rd at a time, to pureed vegetables in a saucepan, stirring gently to mix well. Taste and add salt and pepper if required. When all liquid mixed in, reheat to boiling point stirring gently. Turn off heat and enjoy.

Carrot soup cooked in Crockpot/Slow Cooker.

1 medium Shallot

Potato approx. 100g/4oz

Carrots approx. 230g/8oz

Chicken or vegetable stock cube

Salt and Pepper

Turn Crockpot on to high setting. Boil up a kettle of water and pour approx. 500ml hot water into the crockpot, leave covered for 5 mins. Dissolve stock cube in 500 ml of hot water, carefully taste and season if necessary. Empty out water from crockpot and replace with hot stock.

Peel and slice potato, carrots and shallot and add to stock in crockpot. Stir and leave covered, simmering gently, for 2 hours. Can be turned down to lower setting after an hour but must be simmering well. Vegetables should be quite soft.

Using a slotted spoon, take vegetables from the stock and put them into a bowl. Mash a little with a fork. Pour off liquid into a jug, put aside while you either put vegetables into liquidiser or use a hand blender and whizz for a couple of minutes, alternatively use potato masher and mash well. Return pureed vegetables to crockpot then add liquid 1/3rd at a time, stirring gently to mix well. Taste and add salt and pepper if required. When all liquid is mixed in, cover and leave simmering gently for a few minutes, when it should be ready to enjoy.

Celery soup.

4 sticks Celery

1 medium size Shallot

1 medium size Potato

Chicken stock cube dissolved in 500ml hot water

Knob of butter

Salt and pepper

Trim off ends of celery and discard. wash stalks and slice thinly.
Peel potatoes and cut into small pieces.

Peel shallot and slice.

Put butter into a saucepan and soften over a medium heat. Add potato
pieces and shallot and stir well. Add celery slices and stock and stir
well. Bring to the boil then reduce heat, cover and leave simmering for
15 minutes, or until celery and potatoes are soft. Add more seasoning
if necessary. Strain off liquid into a jug, Put potato and celery mix into
a suitable jug or bowl and whizz with blender until well mixed and
smooth. Return liquid, 1/3rd at a time, to pureed vegetables in
saucepan, stirring gently to mix well. Reheat, then it is ready to serve
and enjoy.

Leek and Potato soup.

Approx.230g/8oz Leek

Approx.230g/8oz Potato

Medium size Shallot

Chicken or vegetable stock cube

Knob of Butter about the size of a walnut

Salt and Pepper

Dissolve stock cube in 500ml hot water.

Trim leek as necessary, slice thinly and chop a little to break it up, place in a colander and rinse in cold water.

Peel potato and cut into small pieces, Peel shallot and slice thinly.

In a medium size saucepan and over a low heat, soften butter then add leek, shallot and potato and stir well. Taste stock, add seasoning if necessary add to saucepan, bring to the boil, reduce heat, cover and leave to simmer, stirring occasionally, for 20 minutes or until potato and leek are soft. Strain off most of liquid into a jug; leave this to one side while you blend the potato and leek for a few minutes. Return liquid, 1/3rd at a time, to pureed vegetables in the saucepan, stirring gently to mix well. Bring to the boil then turn off heat. Season more if necessary. This is ready to serve and enjoy.

Parsnip soup cooked on the hob.

1 medium Shallot

15g/½oz. Butter

Potato approx. 100g/4oz

Parsnips approx. 230g/8oz (2 medium)

Vegetable stock cube dissolved in 500ml hot water

Salt and Pepper to taste.

Peel potato and parsnips and cut them up into small pieces.

Peel shallot and slice.

Place butter in saucepan over a medium heat, add vegetables stir and mix well. Add stock, increase heat and bring to boiling point. Reduce heat and leave, covered, simmering gently, stirring occasionally, until quite soft (approximately 15-20 minutes). Strain off most of the liquid into a jug, put aside while you either put vegetables into liquidiser or use a hand blender and whizz for a couple of minutes. Alternatively use potato masher and mash well. Return liquid, 1/3rd at a time, to pureed vegetables in the saucepan, stirring gently to mix well. Taste and add salt and pepper if required. When all liquid mixed in, reheat to boiling point stirring gently. Turn off heat and enjoy.

Parsnip soup cooked in Crockpot/Slow Cooker.

1 medium Shallot

Potato approx. 100g/4oz

Parsnips approx. 230g/8oz (2 medium)

Vegetable stock cube dissolved in 500ml hot water

Salt and Pepper to taste.

Turn Crockpot on to high setting. Boil up a kettle of water and pour approx. 500ml hot water into the crockpot, leave covered for 5 mins. Dissolve stock cube in 500 ml of hot water, carefully taste and season if necessary. Empty out water from crockpot and replace with hot stock.

Peel and slice potato, parsnips and shallot and add to stock in crockpot. Stir and leave covered, simmering gently, for 2 hours. Can be turned down to lower setting after an hour but must be simmering well. Vegetables should be quite soft.

Using a slotted spoon, take vegetables from the stock and put them into a bowl. Mash a little with a fork. Pour off liquid into a jug, put aside while you either put vegetables into liquidiser or use a hand blender and whizz for a couple of minutes, alternatively use potato masher and mash well. Return pureed vegetables to crockpot then add liquid 1/3rd at a time, stirring gently to mix well. Taste and add salt and pepper if required. When all liquid is mixed in, cover and leave simmering gently for a few minutes, when it should be ready to enjoy.

Vegetable soup cooked on the hob.

Approx. 230g/8oz Cabbage

1 medium size Carrot

1 medium size Parsnip

1 medium size Potato

Veg stock cube

Salt and pepper

Knob of butter

Medium size shallot

Dissolve stock cube in 500ml/1pint hot water.

Remove and discard outside leaves of cabbage, trim off and discard discoloured area of base of stalk, cut away stalk and place in a bowl of cold salted water, shred leaves thinly and leave in bowl with stalk. Peel and trim carrot and parsnip and cut into small pieces. Peel potato and cut into small pieces. Rinse cabbage stalk and cut into small pieces. Peel and slice shallot.

Put butter into a saucepan and over a low to medium heat soften butter then add potato, cabbage stalk, shallot, carrot and parsnip, stir and mix well. Pour in stock, stir well, bring to the boil, reduce heat, cover and leave to simmer. Rinse cabbage leaves and add to the saucepan, stir well, bring back to the boil, reduce heat, cover and leave simmering for 20 minutes or until vegetables are soft. Add salt and pepper if required.

Strain off liquid into a jug. Put vegetables into a suitable jug or bowl and whizz with blender until soft. Return liquid, 1/3rd at a time, to pureed vegetables in the saucepan, stirring gently to mix well. Reheat then it is ready to serve and enjoy.

Vegetable soup cooked in Crockpot/Slow Cooker.

Approx. 230g/8oz Cabbage

1 medium size Carrot

1 medium size Parsnip

1 medium size Potato

Veg stock cube

Salt and pepper

Medium size shallot

Turn Crockpot on to high setting. Boil up a kettle of water and pour approx. 500ml hot water into the crockpot, leave covered for 5 mins. Dissolve stock cube in 500 ml of hot water, carefully taste and season if necessary. Empty out water from crockpot and replace with hot stock.

Discard any discoloured pieces from cabbage trim and cut into small pieces and leave in lightly salted cold water for 5 minutes

Peel and slice potato, carrot, parsnip and shallot and add to stock in crockpot. Rinse cabbage in cold water and add to crockpot. Stir and leave covered, simmering gently, for 2 hours. Can be turned down to lower setting after an hour but must be simmering well. Vegetables should be quite soft.

Using a slotted spoon, take vegetables from the stock and put them into a bowl. Mash a little with a fork. Pour off liquid into a jug, put aside while you either put vegetables into liquidiser or use a hand blender and whizz for a couple of minutes, alternatively use a potato masher and mash well. Return pureed vegetables to crockpot then add liquid

1/3rd at a time, stirring gently to mix well. Taste and add salt and pepper if required. When all liquid is mixed in, cover and leave simmering gently for a few minutes, when it should be ready to serve and enjoy.

Cakes and Puddings

Most of us enjoy cakes and puddings, here are some of my favourite recipes that are easy to make, a treat to eat and not too naughty.

Apple and cinnamon pudding.

Serves 4.

I large or 2 medium cooking apples

30g/1oz Sultanas

1 tablespoon plus 1 teaspoon of Sugar

Knob of Butter about the size of a walnut plus a little for greasing dish

For topping:

1 Egg beaten

60g/2oz Butter

60g/2oz Sugar

60g/2oz Self-raising flour

1 rounded teaspoon ground cinnamon

You will need an ovenproof dish approx. ¾ litre lightly buttered.

Pre heat oven to 200c/400f.

Put mixing bowl to warm over a pan of warm water.

Peel and thinly slice apples.

Put knob of butter in a saucepan, over low heat. Add apple slices and a tablespoon of sugar Stir well for 2 minutes then leave covered, stirring often until apple just begins to soften. Turn off heat and leave covered while you make topping.

Put sugar and butter into warmed mixing bowl, when softened beat together until well mixed and no lumps.

Add 2/3rds of cinnamon to flour and mix well.

Add 2/3rds beaten egg to butter and sugar and beat well together. Add rest of egg with a spoonful of flour, mix well. Carefully add rest of flour and beat well.

Mix sultanas with par cooked apples and put into lightly buttered ovenproof dish.

Spread topping over evenly; make a slight well in centre.

Mix rest of cinnamon with a teaspoon of sugar and spread evenly over top.

Place on a baking tray in pre heated oven and bake for 25 mins or until nicely golden. Reduce heat to 180c and bake for a further 5 mins. If this is to be eaten within the hour, it will be fine to leave it in the oven while oven is cooling down.

Apple and Sultana Crumble.

Serves 4.
500g/18oz Cooking Apples
30g/1oz Sultanas (optional)
30g/1oz Sugar
10g/¼oz Butter

For the crumble topping
100g/4oz Flour
50g/2oz Butter
35g/1¼oz Sugar
25g/1oz Rolled oats

You will need a 1litre ovenproof dish.

Pre heat oven to 190c/375f.
In a mixing bowl rub butter into flour until it resembles fresh breadcrumbs then add sugar and rolled oats and mix well.
Peel apples remove core and slice (Not too thinly). Put butter into a saucepan over a low to medium heat, add apple slices spread sugar evenly over and stir gently for about 5 minutes when apple should be just starting to cook. Put apples into a 1litre ovenproof dish add sultanas if using them. Spread crumble topping evenly over fruit and bake in pre heated oven for 30 minutes or until topping is crisp and golden. Serve with custard, cream or Ice Cream.

Note: *If using a hand pastry blender to rub butter into flour, I find it easier to add sugar before mixing.*

Boiled Fruit Cake.

1 cup Sultanas

1 cup Raisins

1 cup Sugar (Soft brown sugar makes it even more yummy)

2 cups S.R. Flour

1 egg

1 cup water

100g/4oz Butter

Put sultanas, raisins, sugar, water and butter in a saucepan, bring gently to boil, reduce heat and leave to simmer gently for 10-15mins, leave to cool for a few hours.

When thoroughly cool preheat oven to 180c/350f.

Add flour and egg and mix well. Put in to lined 2lb loaf tin and bake in pre heated oven for 1¼ hours or until cooked when tested. (It is worthwhile checking after 1 hour)

You can test by inserting a clean knife (I use a sterilised knitting needle) which should come out clean, if not return cake to oven and cook for another 10 minutes and test again.

Bread and butter pudding.

Serves 4.

3 slices Bread with crusts removed

60g/2oz Butter

85g/3oz Dried fruit (raisins and sultanas mixed)

2 eggs

150ml/1/4 pint milk

Teaspoon vanilla essence

You will need an ovenproof dish approx. ¾ litre.

Spread butter on one side of bread. Cut into halves if using a square dish or 4 triangles if using a round dish.

Lightly butter an ovenproof dish. Arrange a layer of fruit in the bottom then cover with half of the bread spread rest of fruit on top then cover with remaining bread.

Beat eggs in a jug, add milk and vanilla essence and pour over bread and fruit.

Leave to stand for 30min then bake in pre heated oven at 200c/400f for 25 -30 min until top is golden brown.

This is nice served with custard, cream or ice cream.

Carrot and Raisin cake.

100g/3½oz Raisins

170g/6oz S.R. Flour

40g/1½oz Butter softened

140g/5oz Soft Brown Sugar

2 large eggs

100g/4oz Carrots peeled and grated

1 teaspoon Vanilla essence

Line a 2lb loaf tin, set oven at 175c/350f

Put butter, carrots, sugar and raisins into a large mixing bowl and mix well. Beat eggs in jug add vanilla essence then add to bowl and mix well. Add flour into mixture and fold in. Put mixture in to loaf tin and cook for approx. 50mins or until done when tested.

I think it improves flavour if left for 24 hours before eating or freezing. Makes 10 generous slices.

Carrot and raisin Buns (makes 12)

170g/6oz S.R. flour (Wholemeal gives extra flavour)

1 tsp. Ground Cinnamon

150ml/1/4 pint Sunflower oil

140g/5oz Soft Brown Sugar

3 medium eggs

1 tsp vanilla essence

60g/2oz Raisins

230g/8oz Carrots peeled and grated

Set oven 180c/350f.

Place muffin cases in muffin tray.

Mix flour and ground cinnamon in a bowl.

Add oil, sugar, raisins and grated carrot.

Beat eggs in jug add vanilla essence then add to bowl and mix well.

Spoon the mixture into paper cases. Bake for 25-30 mins in pre heated oven until risen and golden. The buns should be fairly firm when pressed lightly in the centre.

Chocolate and Raisin cup-cakes (Makes 12).

175g/6oz Butter

175g/6oz Granulated sugar

3 eggs at room temperature

30g/1oz Cacao or Cocoa powder

140g/5oz S.R. Flour

60g/2oz Raisins

Pre heat oven to 200c/400f.

Line a muffin tin with 12 papers.

In a bowl add Cacao/Cocoa powder to flour and mix well.

In a mixing bowl warm butter; this can be done by placing the mixing bowl over saucepan of hot water. Add sugar and beat with butter until smooth. Beat eggs and add 1 at a time mixing well adding a tablespoon of flour with last egg. Add raisins to flour and Cacao/Cocoa powder. Mix well then add this to mixing bowl. Stir in and mix well.

Put the mixture into prepared muffin tin and bake in pre heated oven for 20 - 25 mins. The cup-cakes should be firm when pressed lightly in the centre.

Just a couple of my homespun poems

With using fresh vegetables I compost all the peelings and now have quite an established compost bin. When I lift the lid I see an army of worms all working away and transforming my kitchen waste into lovely compost.

Sometime ago I lifted the lid and dropped in the outside bits of a cauliflower and as it all landed with a thud on top of all the other stuff in there I thought 'Am I hurting any worms?'

So I sat and penned this poem on behalf of the millions of worms that are beavering away in our compost bins for gardeners everywhere.

Yes I have been told I should get out more.

A Worm's appeal

For all of my life I've lived in this bin
Safe from birds that arrive early or late
You keep us well fed and it's always good stuff
But I'm sad cos I've just lost my mate.

I see the smile on your face as you peer in the top
And see us all working like ants
You know that we're recycling all your kitchen waste
producing compost to put on your plants.

When you lift the lid and bury us each time
With egg shells, cabbage leaves and spud peelings
I wonder, if by chance, has it ever crossed your mind
That even a worm can have feelings?

Last week a whole potato landed on me
Since then my love life has been grim
The worm that I love is a distance away
She prefers the other side of the bin.

I can't wriggle as fast as I used to
And you keep building me mountains to climb
When I reach her I feel so exhausted
She says I'm just wasting my time.

Quite often you look in and give a good stir
And I'm back once again at this end
Do you do this for fun? 'cos I'd like you to know
That it's driving me right round the bend.

Yesterday I decided to cling to the lid
So when you opened it I fell by her side
But the body felt stiff and didn't respond

it appeared that my loved one had died.

I caressed her stiff body and said how I cared
She was the loveliest worm I'd ever known
For me there'd be no other of that I was sure
So I'll spend the rest of my life all alone.

My poor heart was breaking, then I heard her voice
Saying, "What are you doing with that stick?"
She's left me now for an intelligent worm
She tells me that I'm stupid and thick.

So Mr Gardener, may I make a request
For all my friends that live in this bin?
We enjoy the good food that you give us
But could you be more careful how you drop it in?

I have read that poem to many audiences and some people have said that since they heard it they have thought about it each time they have put kitchen waste in their compost bins and have assured me they now do it very carefully. So I added these verses;

Many worms I guess are grateful
For this poem that I wrote
Many gardeners who have heard it
have said they've taken note.

My words have echoed in folks heads
As they've dropped scraps in the bin
They say they now cut things up small
And gently put them in

So when I am departed

And folk list my deeds and sins
I may go down in history
As Patron Saint of compost bins.

And one about my early experience in using my crockpot

The Benefits of Slow cooking and shopping locally.

For many years I had lived by myself
so when cooking for 3 friends or more
I often found the veg were ready to eat
but the meat, in the centre, was raw.

I went for a walk down the High Street
one cold and wet winter's day
from A E. Wallis I bought a slow-cooker
I'd heard it was simple to cook food that way.

Then I went in to my local butcher
I bought stewing steak and vegetables too
and at 11 o'clock the next morning
I prepared myself a stew.

At 6 in the evening, having cooked a few spuds
I lifted the lid of the pot
then served myself a delicious meal
the meat was tender, tasty and hot.

So I invited 3 friends to dinner
I'd cook chicken in lemon and tarragon.
When I put the chicken in the crock-pot
it was too big, the lid wouldn't fit on.

So I had to cut it into pieces
which really spoiled the effect.
Although it was tender and tasty
the presentation didn't really impress.

I'm optimistic and I don't give up hope
so I invited my friends once again
I'd found another recipe for slow cooking
this time for a nice leg of lamb.

So I measured my pot and went to my local butcher
I bought six of his Gret Big Eggs   (Norfolk for great)
I said, "I'd also like a leg of lamb
but there's a favour I would like to beg.

I plan to slow-cook this leg of lamb
so while I would like 3 pounds in weight
the size and shape is important too
could you cut it 3inches by eight?"

So thanks to Alan and my slow cooking pot
the meal really was a success
I'd not been slaving over a hot stove
in fact it had caused me no stress.

Of all the benefits of shopping locally

the most recent one I have found

In supermarkets no one appears to have been taught

how many inches there are in 1lb.

Doreen Reed

Has entertained many audiences with her homespun, thought provoking amusing tales of everyday life, some are nostalgic, some have a twist, and most will make you chuckle.

She is well known as a writer of observational stories, mostly told in rhyme. She is witty, sometimes cheeky, with a down to earth style which anyone who remembers the fifties or sixties can relate to.

Cds and books of some of her poems are available from her website

www.doreenreedpoet.com

Books in paperback and E Book format are available from

Amazon

24927155R00045

Printed in Poland
by Amazon Fulfillment
Poland Sp. z o.o., Wrocław